USING THIS BOOK

*Children learn to read by **reading**, but they need help to begin.*

When you have read the story on the left-hand pages aloud to the child, go back to the beginning of the book and look at the pictures together.

Encourage children to read the sentences under the pictures. If they don't know a word, give them a chance to "guess" what it is from the illustrations before telling them.

There are more suggestions for helping children learn to read in the *Parent/Teacher Guide.*

© Text and layout SHEILA McCULLAGH MCMLXXXV
© In publication LADYBIRD BOOKS LTD MCMLXXXV
Loughborough, England
LADYBIRD BOOKS, INC.
Lewiston, Maine 04240 U.S.A.

Printed in England

Hickory Mouse

written by SHEILA McCULLAGH
illustrated by JON DAVIS

This book belongs to:

_____

Ladybird Books

Chestnut Mouse, Miranda Mouse,
and Jeremy Mouse
were out in the garden
of the big house
at the end of Puddle Lane.

They were eating grass seeds,
when somebody said, "Hi!"
in a very loud voice.

Jeremy Mouse,
Miranda Mouse, and
Chestnut Mouse

They spun around, and saw
another mouse looking at them.
He had a very shiny coat.
He had very bright eyes, and
he had very long whiskers.

"Hello, Hickory," said Chestnut.
"That's a funny name," said Jeremy.
"What's **your** name?" asked Hickory.
"My name's Jeremy," said Jeremy.
"And mine's Miranda," said Miranda.

Hickory Mouse

Hickory burst out laughing.
"Jeremy!" he cried. "Miranda!
You're called Jeremy and Miranda,
and you think **my** name's funny!"
And he laughed so hard, that
he had to hold his sides.
"All mice who live in the woods
are named after trees," said Chestnut.
"Hickory is a kind of tree."
"But Chestnut's a nut," said Miranda.
"Chestnuts grow on chestnut trees,"
said Chestnut.

Miranda, Jeremy,
Chestnut, and Hickory

The three little mice stood watching,
until at last Hickory stopped laughing.
"Are you eating grass seeds?"
he asked, scornfully. "You come with me,
and we'll go to Puddle Lane,
and find some cheese."

"It's dangerous in Puddle Lane,"
said Chestnut. "It's much safer,
here in the garden."
"Hah!" said Hickory, scornfully.
"You're afraid! I'm brave!
You come with me and I'll show you
just how brave a mouse can be!"

Hickory said, ''You come with me.
We will go to Puddle Lane,
and find some cheese.''

Hickory turned around,
and saw the Griffle.
The Griffle was standing
by the gate.
He was looking down Puddle Lane.
Hickory ran up onto a rock.
"Hi!" squeaked Hickory,
as loudly as he could squeak.

The Griffle was a friendly monster,
but he was afraid of mice.
He looked around.
He saw Hickory—
and he vanished!

The Griffle was by the gate.
The Griffle saw Hickory.
The Griffle vanished.

Hickory laughed so hard, that
tears came to his eyes.
He danced around on top of the rock.
He was so pleased with himself,
that he began to sing.
He made up the song as he went along.

"I'm the bravest mouse,
I'm the bravest mouse!
I'm dancing on a rock.
My name is Hickory,
Hickory-Dickory,
Hickory-Dickory-Dock!"

Hickory sang,
''I'm the bravest mouse,
I'm the bravest mouse!
I'm dancing on a rock.
My name is Hickory,
Hickory-Dickory,
Hickory-Dickory-Dock!''

Hickory liked his song so much,
that he sang it all over again.
Then he ran to the gate, and
went out into Puddle Lane.
"Come on!" he called to the others.
"Follow me!"

Mrs. Pitter-Patter was standing
in Puddle Lane.
She was outside Mr. Gotobed's house.
She was bending down, and
looking in through the keyhole.

Hickory saw Mrs. Pitter-Patter.
Mrs. Pitter-Patter
was outside Mr. Gotobed's house.

Hickory ran to the doorway of
Mr. Gotobed's house, and climbed
up to the top of the lock,
just above the keyhole.
"Hi!" squeaked Hickory,
as loudly as he could squeak.
Mrs. Pitter-Patter looked up.
There was Hickory Mouse,
right in front of her nose!

Mrs. Pitter-Patter looked up.
She saw Hickory Mouse.

"Help!" cried Mrs. Pitter-Patter.
"Help! Help! A mouse!"
She ran away down Puddle Lane
as fast as she could run.
She ran into her own house,
and shut the door with a bang.

"Help!" cried Mrs. Pitter-Patter.
"Help! Help! A mouse!"
Mrs. Pitter-Patter
ran down Puddle Lane
as fast as she could run.

Hickory laughed so hard, that
the tears ran out of his eyes,
and down to his whiskers.
He danced around on the top of the lock,
and began to sing his song.

"I'm the bravest mouse,
I'm the bravest mouse!
I'm dancing on a lock.
My name is Hickory,
Hickory-Dickory,
Hickory-Dickory-Dock!"

Hickory sang,
"I'm the bravest mouse,
I'm the bravest mouse!
I'm dancing on a lock.
My name is Hickory,
Hickory-Dickory,
Hickory-Dickory-Dock!"

The other three mice stood watching him,
until at last he stopped dancing
and looked down.
"The window is open," he said.
"I'm going inside,
to look for some cheese."
Hickory slipped in through
the open window.

Hickory saw the open window.
"I'm going in," he said.

Jeremy looked at Chestnut.
"Let's go too," he said. "I'm hungry."
"Let's go and watch
from the window sill," said Chestnut.

The three little mice
climbed up to the window sill,
and looked in.

The three little mice
looked in.

Mr. Gotobed was fast asleep
in his chair by the fire.
He was snoring gently in his sleep.
Hickory Mouse was sitting on a stool
right in front of him.
"Hi!" squeaked Hickory,
as loudly as he could squeak.
"Hi! Hi! Hi!"
But Mr. Gotobed snored on.

Mr. Gotobed was fast asleep,
in his chair by the fire.

Hickory looked around.
There was a tall grandfather clock
standing against the wall.
Hickory ran over to the clock,
and climbed up to the very top.

He began to dance
on the top of the clock,
and as he danced, he sang.

"I'm the bravest mouse,
I'm the bravest mouse!
I'm dancing on the clock.
My name is Hickory,
Hickory-Dickory,
Hickory-Dickory-Dock!"

Hickory sang,
"I'm the bravest mouse,
I'm the bravest mouse!
I'm dancing on the clock.
My name is Hickory,
Hickory-Dickory,
Hickory-Dickory-Dock!"

The wheels inside the clock
began to whir.

Ding-dong, ding-dong,
ding-dong, ding-dong,
went the clock.

Ding-dong, ding-dong,
ding-dong, ding-dong.
DONG!

The clock struck one.
The clock shook with the sound.

The clock struck one.
Dong!

Hickory Mouse was so frightened,
that he couldn't move.
He stood still on the top of the clock,
as if he had turned to stone.

Mr. Gotobed gave a great snort,
and woke up.
He saw Hickory.
He sat up in his chair.

Mr. Gotobed woke up.
He saw Hickory.
He sat up in his chair.

35

Hickory fled.
He ran down the clock,
and across the floor.
He ran up the wall to the window.
He pushed his way past
the three little mice,
and ran down the wall.
He ran off down Puddle Lane,
as fast as he could run.

Jeremy, Chestnut, and Miranda
ran down the wall into the lane,
and back into the Magician's garden.

Hickory ran away.
He ran off down Puddle Lane,
as fast as he could run.

"Well!" said Mr. Gotobed.
"Well! Well! Well!"
He began to laugh.
Then he began to sing,
"Hickory-Dickory-Dock!
The mouse ran up the clock.
The clock struck one.
The mouse ran down.
Hickory-Dickory-Dock."

Mr. Gotobed sang,
"Hickory-Dickory-Dock!
The mouse ran up the clock.
The clock struck one.
The mouse ran down.
Hickory-Dickory-Dock."

Songs about Hickory Mouse

When you read this story, sing the songs to the child. You can make up a tune as you go along (as Hickory did), or just say the words in a singsong voice, stressing the rhythm.

Children enjoy rhymes, and usually remember them, so after they have heard the story, they will probably be able to "read" the words of the songs on the right-hand pages.

If they can't, then sing or read the songs to them again, running your finger under the words as you do so, and encouraging them to join in.

"I'm the bravest mouse,
I'm the bravest mouse!
I'm dancing on a clock.
My name is Hickory,
Hickory-Dickory,
Hickory-Dickory-Dock!"

Hickory-Dickory-Dock,
The mouse ran up the clock.
The clock struck one.
The mouse ran down.
Hickory-Dickory-Dock!

Look at the pictures, and read the words.

rock

lock

clock

Notes for the parent/teacher

Turn back to the beginning, and print the child's name in the space on the title page, using ordinary, not capital letters.

Now go through the book again. Look at each picture and talk about it. Point to the caption below, and read it aloud yourself.

Run your finger under the words as you read, so that the child learns that reading goes from left to right.

Encourage the child to read the words under the illustrations. Don't rush in with the word before he/she has had time to think, but don't leave him/her struggling.

Read this story as often as the child likes hearing it. The more opportunities he/she has to look at the illustrations and **read** the captions with you, the more he/she will come to recognize the words.

If you have several books, let the child choose which story he/she would like.

Mrs Pitter-Patte... dropped the tail with a ye... She made such a noise, that she woke Mr Gotobed, who was fast asleep in bed in the house at the end of the lane.

Mr. Gotobed woke up.